Original title:
By the Coral Shores

Copyright © 2025 Creative Arts Management OÜ
All rights reserved.

Author: Elias Marchant
ISBN HARDBACK: 978-1-80581-517-4
ISBN PAPERBACK: 978-1-80581-044-5
ISBN EBOOK: 978-1-80581-517-4

Beneath the Surface Whisper

The fish wore hats, so very fine,
They danced on bubbles, sipped their wine.
A crab played chess with a dolphin sleek,
While octopuses sang, all in a week.

Starfish competed in a limbo game,
With seaweed swaying, oh what a claim!
A turtle rode a wave like a boss,
While jellyfish giggled, their laughter, a toss.

Lighthouses in Twilight

Lighthouses blinked like a disco ball,
Seabirds grooved, answer the call.
A lighthouse keeper wore bright pink socks,
And danced with sea turtles, oh what a shock!

The tide rolled in with a giggling sound,
As clams hummed low, swaying around.
A seagull tried to take a selfie,
With a crab that grinned, feeling quite wealthy.

Tides of the Heart

The tide pulled back with a cheeky grin,
Shells whispered secrets, oh let's dive in!
A starfish winked, said, 'Join the fun,'
While sandcastles melted under the sun.

Crabs juggled shells, all in good jest,
While an anemone danced, feeling blessed.
A seahorse rode a wave with flair,
Sprinkling laughter all in the air.

Ventures in the Waves

A whale wore sunglasses, feeling so cool,
Swimming past fish who broke every rule.
Dolphins played tag, racing with glee,
While sea turtles floated, sipping sweet tea.

Bubbles burst forth like tiny balloons,
Crabs tripped over their own silly tunes.
A sea cucumber slipped on a sand,
And mermaids laughed, with joy so grand.

Salty Breezes and Haunting Calls

The seagulls squawk their morning shout,
One stole my sandwich, that's no doubt!
Crabs in pajamas dance on the sand,
Who knew crustaceans could be so grand?

A fish did a flip and splashed me good,
I fell on my back, it's not what I could!
Turtles in shades sunbathing slow,
Thinking they're models, putting on a show!

The Color of Ocean Depths

The waves are laughing in shades of blue,
I dipped my toes, oh, what a view!
A jellyfish waved like a floating balloon,
I shouted in joy—till it stung like a tune!

Paddleboards surf past, with glee and a splash,
One dude just fell; oh, what a crash!
Underwater, the fish play peek-a-boo,
While I'm out here forgetting my shoe!

Sheltered Amongst the Rocks

Amongst the rocks, crabs set a feast,
With seaweed for garnish, it's a gooey beast!
Starfish are plotting a takeover plan,
While I'm just trying to kick up some sand!

A clam yelled, "Dinner!" but found no plate,
So it sat and sulked, feigning fate.
The tide rolled in, bringing laughter and cheer,
I just hope the fish can't hear my beer!

Harmonies of the Surf

The surf sings tunes of a bubbly delight,
While kids build castles that vanish in sight.
A wave crashed hard, right into my hat,
The ocean mocked me with a splashy spat!

Seagulls are crooning in natural jest,
Their dive-bombing antics put humor to test.
As shells compete for the best little song,
I laugh at the sand, where I surely belong!

Whispers of the Tidal Embrace

The seagulls squawk a silly tune,
While starfish dance beneath the moon.
A lobster's lost his way to lunch,
And seahorses prance in a goofy hunch.

Crabs wear hats, oh what a sight,
They strut like kings, with all their might.
A clam once tried to tell a joke,
But all it did was make me choke!

Beneath the Waves' Serenade

Bubbles rise as fish play tag,
A dolphin laughs, it's quite a brag.
With seaweed hair, the mermaids sing,
Their tales of treasures, and silly bling.

A shrimp once fished for his own feet,
In hopes to find a tasty treat.
But all he got was a crab's pinch,
Now he's not laughing, not an inch!

Echoes of the Seaside Dream

A turtle's race, oh what a show,
He took a nap, then moved real slow.
The waves they sing, with a wink and grin,
But watch your toes, here comes a fin!

A porpoise jokes with a splash and flip,
While jellyfish glide with an elegant dip.
Oh, the antics of friends in the surf,
Bring endless giggles and lots of mirth!

The Dance of Barnacles and Sunlight

Barnacles have a dance-off, do you see?
With barnacle boys and girls in glee.
A fish in a hat tells jokes with flair,
But it's the anemones that steal the air.

The sea cucumber couldn't find a date,
He asked a clam, but it just ate.
So in the waves, they laugh and play,
Under the sun, all day, hooray!

The Call of the Shell-Kissed Rocks

Upon the rocks, the seashells chatter,
A crab in a hat claims it's all a matter.
The seagulls squawk, oh what a show,
Arguing who gets the best shell to throw.

Waves tickle toes, a slippery dance,
A fish flops by as if in a trance.
Seashells giggle, they jostle and jive,
What a ruckus, the ocean comes alive!

Starlit Waters and Sandy Shores

Beneath the stars, the tide pulls tight,
A dolphin shows off, what a funny sight!
Sandcastles tumble, the tide is a tease,
"Invasion!" they scream, as they crumble with ease.

Laughter echoes, the night is bright,
Flashlights flicker, a curious sight.
A crab is the judge, it's quite the affair,
Waving his claws, like he just doesn't care!

The Palette of Driftwood and Dune

Driftwood reclines, a lazy display,
Telling tall tales of ships gone astray.
A piece of old rope gives a half-hearted sigh,
"It was quite the adventure," it claims with a lie.

Colors of sand on a painter's brush,
Seagulls throw paint with a reckless rush.
The dunes giggle, they shift and they sway,
"The art of the shore, come join our ballet!"

Secrets Carried by the Sea Breeze

The breeze brings secrets, whispers in flight,
A seaweed wiggles, oh what a sight!
It tells of fish that wear fancy hats,
And turtles that dance with the beachside rats.

Sand dollars clink like coins in a game,
"Pick me!" they shout, "I'm rich with fame!"
But when the tide knocks, they scatter away,
"Oh no! Not again, it's another 'buggy day'!"

Tales from the Ocean's Edge

There once was a crab with a hat,
He danced with a clam and a cat.
They twirled on the sand,
In a wacky band of pelagic acrobat!

A fish with a grin, oh so wide,
Drove a sea turtle to madness, they tried.
With bubbles galore,
They splashed and they swore, 'We're the best at this tide!'

A dialogue surfaced with the seaweed,
Who chirped 'I can sing; yes, indeed!'
But tangled in knots,
He forgot all his thoughts, 'Just let me proceed!'

In the shadows, a starfish proclaimed,
That prancing and dancing was famed.
With laughter laid bare,
They enjoyed sunny air, until they all named their game!

The Gentle Caress of Coastal Whispers

Oh the whispers of breeze make me chuckle,
As seagulls dive down with a shuffle.
They pester the sand,
While the sun takes a stand, 'You're ruffling my trouble!'

A seal held a party on rock,
With a conch shell as loud as a clock.
They danced with the tide,
While the octopus tried, 'Now that's quite the shock!'

The crabs laughed at a starfish's fall,
As he tripped on a soft jelly ball.
With a wink and a nudge,
A flip and a grudge, 'What's hap-'pened to all?'

In the distance, the waves start to crash,
As kelp gives a most amusing splash.
Nature's own jest,
In the ocean's fine fest, keeps me laughing in a flash!

Dance of the Tide-Pool Spirits

The tide pools are bustling with glee,
Where a shrimp plays the ukulele like me.
They strum and they sway,
In a watery way, 'Oh look at that jellyfish flee!'

A sea snail wearing gold-rimmed specs,
Declared that he's up next for checks.
He spun in a trance,
Taking quite the chance—'I'm no ordinary hex!'

Anemones groove to the beat,
As they sway on their colorful seat.
With drumming from shells,
And laughter that swells, 'This party's a tidal retreat!'

With all of its creatures in line,
The sea otters raised their sweet wine.
They toasted and cheered,
For the fun that appeared, 'Our coastal ballet is divine!'

Moonlit Dreams of the Sea

Under the moon, the dolphins prance,
They splash in the waves, oh what a dance!
With laughter that glows,
And a glimmering prose, 'Come join us in our moonlit trance!'

A clam told a tale of the night,
Of a pirate who lost his last fight.
With patches and scars,
And dreams that flew far, he claimed he could still see the light!

A quirky fish in a polka-dot tie,
Said 'Why not just learn how to fly?'
With bubbles that burst,
And the laughter well-versed, they all gave a resounding high!

As tides winked, beneath silver rays,
Creatures danced through the salty haze.
In a whimsy parade,
Where the night never fade, they all sang their whimsical lays!

Harmonies of the Deep

Fish in tuxedos dance and swirl,
Crabs tell jokes with a sideways twirl.
The octopus plays the ukulele,
While seahorses sing quite fray-lee.

The starfish claps with its five hands,
As dolphins join in with silly plans.
A whale in a top hat takes a bow,
Cheering from each clam and cow.

They giggle and frolic in the sun,
With bubbles rising, oh what fun!
A seaweed band strikes up a tune,
While the jellyfish boogies 'neath the moon.

So come and join this wacky crew,
Where every wave has something new.
In depths where laughter never dies,
Even the mermaids chuckle and sigh.

Embracing the Shore's Edge

Seagulls squabble over a crumb,
While crabs march like army chum.
A beach ball bounces, sails in flight,
And sunscreen fights the urge to bite.

Turtles race in slow-motion glee,
"Catch me if you can!" shouts a bee.
The waves each giggle, swishing like hair,
As sandcastles topple without a care.

A picnic spreads with sandwiches wide,
But ants declare war on each side!
There's laughter in the salty air,
As beachgoers toss frisbees everywhere.

When the sun dips low and lights the bay,
Seashells whisper tales of play.
As the tide rolls in with mischievous cheer,
The shore invites all, come lend an ear.

The Tranquil Meeting of Land and Sea

The waves tiptoe softly on the sand,
Tickling toes as if they planned.
Pelicans dive with clumsy grace,
Making all the fish lose face.

A hermit crab dons a fancy shoe,
While sea turtles act like they're too cool.
The breeze brings whispers, secrets to share,
"A starfish can't dance, but it doesn't care!"

Seashells gather for a raucous chat,
About the best place for sunbathing fat.
And then they giggle, a chorus of sound,
While the waves clamor, swirling around.

As day gives way to evening's glow,
The beach throws a party, don't be slow!
With laughter that carries far and wide,
Where land and sea meet, fun will abide.

Melodies of the Misty Coast

Waves chuckled softly, what a sight,
Seagulls wearing hats, feeling bright.
Crabs in formation, marching along,
Whistling to the rhythm of a silly song.

Shells gossip loudly, sharing their tales,
Turtles play poker, swapping their scales.
Dancing in circles, the fish join the jest,
Making the ocean their comedy fest.

The sand tickles toes, oh what a game,
Sandcastles wobble, they're never the same.
With laughter like bubbles, rising so free,
Creatures unite for a grand jubilee.

Even the octopus joins in the mirth,
Painting the moon with colors of earth.
The mist brings a giggle, whispers of fun,
Leaving behind echoes long after it's done.

Yearning for the Sea's Choir

At dawn, the sea sings a tune so sweet,
Seashells clapping along with their beat.
Mermaids are giggling, a splash in the air,
Jumping on dolphins, without a care.

Barnacles hum tunes in chorus and rhyme,
Crab families dance, oh what a time!
Eels twist and turn in a slippery race,
Waving their fins, making a funny face.

Waves burble laughter as they foam and spray,
Splashing the sails of boats at play.
Fish with sunglasses, a sight to behold,
Strutting their stuff, oh my, so bold!

With seaweeds swaying, the show must go on,
Under the sun, til the curtain's drawn.
Every creature joins in this oceanic spree,
Yearning for laughter of the deep blue sea.

Storms and Stillness

The clouds rumble loud, like a grumpy cat,
Raindrops tap dance, oh what a spat!
Crabs in a war zone, pinching with might,
As waves play tag in the fading light.

Thunder joins in, but the fish just grinned,
Rolling with laughter as the boat spin.
Seagulls stacked high on a tiny old post,
Yelling, "We're flying! Who needs to coast?"

Then calm settles in, like a cozy blanket,
Turtles poke heads out, what a pranklet!
The sun peeks through, sharing sweet smiles,
Waves whisper secrets and humor a while.

A big ol' octopus making a pie,
With ingredients stolen as seagulls fly by.
Laughter erupts as the stillness won't stay,
A hysterical dance in the oceanic ballet.

The Ocean's Timeless Heart

In the heart of the ocean, where secrets reside,
Starfish tell stories of the current tide.
Worms writhe in giggles, dancing along,
Echoing dreams with a buoyant throng.

The jellyfish jive, with a bouncy flair,
Twinkling with laughter, bright colors in air.
With shells as their stage, the crabs strut around,
While sea cucumbers bob on the ground.

Anemones sway, oh what a delight,
In this wild circus, it feels just right.
Tangled up seaweed creates a grand show,
Making sure everyone joins in the flow.

The ocean's heart beats to a rhythm divine,
With comical antics that sparkle and shine.
Forever will the waves spin their playful art,
In this endless dance of the ocean's own heart.

Mosaic of Pebbles and Seaweed

A crab plays tag with a lazy fish,
The sand tickles toes, oh what a wish!
A hermit shell wearing quite a hat,
Laughing at seagulls, oh imagine that!

On the shore, the seaweed dances tall,
Whispering secrets, a muddled sprawl.
Pebbles join in a merry parade,
While gulls perform acrobatics, unafraid!

Here come the tourists, with ice cream cones,
Slipping and sliding, oh those clumsy tones!
Sandcastles crumble like dreams on a breeze,
While everyone's hopping to dodge the deep seas!

A rainbow of shells sings a funny tune,
Under the sun, all the laughter blooms.
With beach balls bouncing, oh what a sight,
The ocean chuckles, all day and night!

Secrets Lurking in the Blue

Bubbles rise up, with secrets galore,
A starfish whispers behind a closed door.
Eels have a giggle, so sly and sleek,
While the ocean decides, it's time for a peek!

The fishes all gather for a wacky show,
Like seaweed dancers putting on quite a glow.
Turtles waddle in, with shades on their eyes,
Declaring themselves the kings of surprise!

Shells clutter the beach, an artistic mess,
Each one a treasure, though none will confess.
Crabs tell tall tales, while flipping their claws,
Joking about the fisherman's silly flaws!

But don't be deceived, there's fun all around,
With laughter and splashes, adventure is found.
As waves crash and sparkle, it's clear to see,
The secrets of water bring giggles and glee!

Lullabies of the Seafoam

As the waves crash down, they hum a sweet tune,
To the flickers of sunlight, afternoon boon.
Seafoam whispers softly, a cradle of cheer,
Rocking the shells, all nestled near!

Fishes bob up, with a wink and a grin,
Playing hide and seek where the bubbles begin.
Barnacles perform in their crusty attire,
While crabs hold a rave, we're all set to retire!

The stars up above twinkle down with delight,
While the moon giggles soft, casting silver light.
With lullabies flowing from the ocean's heart,
Every gentle wave is a magical part!

So close your eyes tight and drift off to dream,
Where seafoam and laughter blend perfectly, it seems.
In this watery wonder, joy never leaves,
Just snuggle up close to the songs of the seas!

Saline Kisses

Salty kisses dance on the breeze,
While fish steal glances with giggles and ease.
The beach ball rolls like a round little chap,
As seagulls toss jokes, with a flap and a flap!

Sunburnt tourists sport flamingo hats,
Chasing beach umbrellas and friendly spats.
The tides play tricks, tickling sand beneath,
While the ocean roars laughter, a gleeful wreath!

Sandy snacks scatter, all over the place,
A crab tries to join with the funniest grace.
Kite-flying dolphins join in on the fun,
As salty waves crash, oh, we've just begun!

At day's end, we chuckle at memories so bright,
With beads of joy shining gold in the light.
As we dip our toes where the waters kiss,
Let's treasure these moments, oh what pure bliss!

Salty Tongues and Winding Paths

Crabs in sunglasses strut with flair,
Gossiping fish without a care.
Seagulls argue who has the best snack,
While dolphins plot their next silly prank.

Tide pools teem with laughter and glee,
Starfish tell tales from under the sea.
Waves crash jokes that tickle the sand,
As clams chime in with a cheeky stand.

Lanterns on the Dune

Sandcastles built to reach the sky,
Mice in cool outfits scurry by.
The sun winks down with a playful grin,
As crabs dance to a tune of sin.

Night falls softly, lanterns gleam,
The moon joins in, a blushing beam.
Mermaids giggle with shells on their heads,
While sea turtles tease those still in beds.

The Coral Whisperers

Coral reefs sharing secrets profound,
In whispers that tickle the ocean bound.
Anemones giggle with every swell,
While octopuses weave a funny spell.

Fish in bow ties debate the trends,
With sea cucumbers claiming they're friends.
A puffer fish boasts of his fine attire,
As clownfish jest with playful fire.

Seaglass Moments

Pieces of stories washed ashore,
Finding treasure is never a bore.
Each shard holds laughter of waves gone past,
Chasing each other in a splashing cast.

A pelican shares tales with a grin,
Of snacks that were lost in the raucous din.
Kids build dreams in the golden tide,
While sandfly concerts take you for a ride.

The Sea's Gentle Embrace

A crab in a tuxedo scuttles by,
Dancing with a seagull, oh me, oh my!
The waves giggle softly, a watery tease,
While starfish whisper secrets in the breeze.

The fish wear sunglasses, looking quite cool,
While jellyfish waltz, breaking every rule.
A turtle in flip-flops joins in the fun,
With every splash, a new joke's begun.

Sandcastles wobble, then tumble with flair,
As kids burst in laughter, forgetting their care.
The ocean chuckles, a mischievous friend,
Where each wave brings joy that never will end.

Currents of Time

The clock ticks slowly, lost in a wave,
Where fish tell tales of the things they crave.
A dolphin jumps high, aiming for a star,
And mermaids laugh loudly from near and far.

Seashells gossip, each one with a tale,
A pirate's treasure, or a whale's big scale.
Sand dollars chuckle at strange, shy fish,
All swims and glimmers, just granting a wish.

Time here is silly, like bubbles that float,
With every splish-splash, we're buoyed with hope.
The ocean is winking, a playful old clock,
In currents of laughter, we all take stock.

Reflections in the Tidepool

In a tidepool's mirror, crabs do a dance,
While a sea cucumber's lost in a trance.
A shrimp with bling shows off what's in vogue,
As a clam rolls its eyes, feeling quite rogue.

Anemones wriggle, all colors and quirks,
As tiny fish giggle; oh, how the joy lurks!
The tides bring a riddle, a splashy delight,
With each little wave, the world feels just right.

Reflecting the laughter, the ocean's own grin,
With starfish performing their grand ol' spin.
In this quirky pool where the weird is embraced,
Every creature is smiling, in joy they're encased.

Sandcastles and Wishes

With buckets and shovels, we each build our dreams,
While seagulls pass by, sharing mischievous schemes.
A fortress of sand with a moat made of foam,
As waves play tag, calling each one 'home'.

While wishes are whispered, in grains they'll slip,
A sandman lounges, oh what a trip!
He grants only giggles, not serious things,
Like hats made of seaweed or tricycles with wings.

As laughter erupts from each castle's high tower,
The ocean's approval arrives with a shower.
In this sandy kingdom where dreams can roam free,
We cherish each moment, just you, and the sea.

Hidden Gems of the Coast

Sandy toes and clumsy falls,
Crabs scuttle as laughter calls.
Sunburned noses, hats askew,
Finding shells is what we do.

Seagulls squawking, stealing fries,
Watch your food, or lose to lies.
Kids in waves, splashes abound,
Splashing laughter all around.

Buried treasures in the sand,
A rusty spoon, a candy hand.
What's that shining? Oh, it's junk!
But we're the kings of beachy funk!

Beach ball fights and iced cold drinks,
Frog catching ends, oh how it stinks!
We'll dance with shadows, sun's a blast,
Making memories that will last.

Where the Sky Meets the Sea

Clouds like cotton candy fluff,
Waves that laugh and play quite tough.
Here I stand, a seagull's throne,
Windy hair, I'm not alone.

Kites like fish fly high above,
Tangled lines, oh, where's the love?
Sailboats drift with tipsy grace,
A pirate's life, let's win this race!

Tanning styles that twist and bend,
Oops! My towel is now a friend.
Sunscreen mishaps, slippery hands,
Making art on shifting sands.

As the sunset paints the skies,
We'll giggle at our funny highs.
Palm trees sway, it's time to roam,
Together on this sandy dome!

Flotsam and Jetsam Tales

Lost and found, a sock appears,
What a prize to start our cheers!
A bottle bobbles, fills with sand,
"Message inside?" we lend a hand.

Old flip-flops, what a pair,
One's all there, the other's rare!
Treasure chests of seaweed stew,
Who knew ocean bits were crew?

Starfish waving, saying hi,
"Take me home!" we hear them cry.
Ten crabs marching in a line,
Who knew crustaceans could combine?

With every tide, new quirks arise,
We gather stories, and surprise!
Flotsam finds from coast to coast,
We're all just seaweed's jolly host.

Driftwood Diaries

Once upon a piece of wood,
A tale begins; it's understood.
Rides the waves, it's quite a show,
Let's write the stories only we know!

A seagull's nest, it tells the tale,
Of beachside shenanigans, and sail.
Sand between toes, giggles erupt,
Driftwood knows when life's abrupt.

Fishy whispers in the breeze,
Tinkle laughter, ocean tease.
Forgotten dreams on splintered beams,
Crafting all our goofy schemes.

Every summer, tales unfold,
Silly moments to be retold.
So grab a stick, let's start to write,
Driftwood's diary, pure delight!

Ocean's Edge Reverie

Seagulls squawk with great delight,
Sandy hats take off in flight.
Crabs dance with a silly sway,
As beach balls bounce and play.

Sunburned noses, gleeful screams,
Ice cream drips ruin beachy dreams.
Kids build castles, but they fall,
A wave comes in, it's a free-for-all!

Turtles in shades, trying to chill,
Waves crash down, giving a thrill.
Surfboards scatter, laughter roars,
As life guards wrestle with beach chores.

Just a day at the edge of fun,
Barefoot runners, on the run.
Belly flop contests make a splash,
Life's a beach, and what a bash!

The Call of the Distant Waves

Whales sing songs to the seagull crew,
While dolphins juggle, oh what a view!
Floating in the salty breeze,
Sailor hats dance with such ease.

Clams hide pearls, but they trick more,
They snap at toes, oh what a roar!
Tide pools bubble, making a fuss,
Cranky octopus joins the bus!

Sharks in sunglasses swim so cool,
And starfish play hopscotch as a rule.
The seaweed sways like a bad hair day,
And jellyfish float on their lazy way.

Surfboards tumble, laughter spills,
Tidal waves hiding all the thrills.
A fish in a tux, oh what a sight!
Join the wave, it's a pure delight!

Love Letters from the Sea

Mermaids write with mussel shells,
Their ink is squid; it surely gels.
They send messages with a splash,
While sea turtles make a dash.

Old sailors dream of love so grand,
Whispers caught in the ocean's hand.
A crab in a tux, looking so neat,
Tries to woo fish with his moves on the street.

Conch shells echo sweet romance,
While bright fish compete for a dance.
Seashells clack in a rhythmic beat,
As dolphins waltz, oh what a treat!

Octopus dates with eight-armed flair,
In seaweed gardens, love fills the air.
A coral kiss, oh so whimsical,
Who knew the sea could be so comical?

Maritime Meditations

Float like a buoy, drift like a log,
Wonder if fish think, or just jog?
The sea is deep, but oh so loud,
Jellyfish float in a noodle crowd.

Sailors ponder life, drink from a cup,
But it spills over when they get up.
Mermaids giggle, splashing around,
While seaweed does a wobbly sound.

Waves whisper secrets to the sand,
As snails creep slowly, oh so bland.
What's life if not a big sea jest?
Flip a shell, and just take a rest.

Laughter echoes from shore to shore,
Where every wave brings tales galore.
Funny thoughts in salty dreams,
Life's a whirl, or so it seems!

Tides of Forgotten Secrets

In the waves, a tattlefish roams,
Whispering tales of octopus homes.
Starfish gossip on sandy beds,
While crabs debate on who'll lose heads.

The tide rolls in with a teapot cheer,
Shells in a circle, the gossip's clear.
Lobsters dance in a crustacean jig,
As sea cucumbers tease a playful dig.

A dolphin dives, a rogue in disguise,
Winks at the gulls, hidden in the skies.
The waves roll laughter like hiccups at play,
Secrets lost; they drift far away.

A Symphony of Salty Breezes

The wind strums tunes on a seashell lute,
While jellyfish waltz in their squishy suit.
Crabs conduct with their pincers raised,
As dolphins leap in a water ballet.

Seagulls squawk in a cacophony bright,
Requesting snacks, what a bold flight!
The sand plays bass with a rhythmic beat,
As shrimp tap dance with their tiny feet.

A surfer stumbles onto a wave,
Hoping for glory, but finds a grave.
Laughter erupts from the salty crowd,
As they cheer for the one who just bowed.

Coral Gardens in Twilight

In twilight's glow, a crab wears a hat,
Chasing a mermaid who's quite a brat.
The corals are giggling, what a sight,
While fish wink gossip in dim twilight.

Seahorses prance as if in a ball,
Their tails intertwined like ribbons that sprawl.
Clownfish chuckle, mischief their art,
While sea stars play games, a nightly chart.

Anemones sway, a chorus divine,
As hermit crabs sneak, in search of a shrine.
What treasures they find in the night's embrace,
With laughter and silliness, they set the pace.

Secrets Beneath the Surf

Beneath the waves, the whispers arise,
Of hidden treasures and fishy lies.
A clam with a secret, a pearl in its grip,
Plans a surprise for a passing ship.

A turtle tells tales of a lost sailor,
Who swam with sharks and sought a trailer.
The octopus nods, all seven arms crossed,
"His ship was made of spaghetti, now lost!"

The seaweed rolls high with giggles of glee,
As sea urchins gossip, "Will we ever be free?"
The ocean's ensemble, a comical chase,
Where laughter and secrets set the pace!

The Dance of Coral Gardens

In the reefs where fish do twirl,
Clownfish wiggle, giving a whirl.
Seaweed sways, like it's got moves,
Even starfish surely approves!

Turtles glide with graceful flair,
While crabs pinch without a care.
A dolphin's laugh, a joyous sound,
In this party, fun abounds!

Seahorses prance, with tiny kicks,
They've got rhythm, and a few tricks.
The ocean floor is quite the stage,
Where every creature turns a page.

So if you seek a merry dance,
Come join the critters, take a chance!
With bubbles bursting, laughter flies,
Underwater, joy never dies!

Legacy of the Ocean Floor

In the depths where sands do play,
Old shells gossip night and day.
A starfish claims it's king for life,
While oysters argue, full of strife.

A crab named Larry, quite the show,
Tells tales of tides and undertow.
He says, 'I once outsmarted a fish!'
But I'm not sure that's his only wish.

Mollusks brag about their pearls,
While seagulls try to steal their swirls.
It's quite the mix down in the gloom,
Where laughter echoes through the room!

Oh, to hear their funny lore,
The ocean's tales forever soar.
Among the driftwood and the foam,
These underwater pals call home.

Heartbeats of the Waves

When the waves crash, hear them cheer,
Salty kisses, spreading good cheer.
A fish with a joke, it flips with glee,
Stirring up laughter under the sea.

The sea urchins chuckle, spikes held high,
While jellyfish glide, oh so sly.
They twirl and twist, like they're on a spree,
Lighting up the ocean mysteriously.

Conch shells echo, tales of the deep,
Of parties thrown, then drifting to sleep.
A whale does a flip, what a delight,
Under the moon, shining bright!

So listen close, and take a dive,
With giggles and splashes, feel alive.
The heartbeats of waves, a joyful hum,
In this watery world, laughter won't be numb!

Chasing the Setting Sun

As daylight fades, the sea's aglow,
Fish race home, putting on a show.
With rocky cliffs, they laugh and play,
Chasing the sun, all night and day.

A pelican drops, with a goofy plop,
While crabs practice their sideways hop.
Frolicking dolphins, with a grin,
Are the real stars, ready to spin!

The horizon blushes, a colorful hue,
While sea turtles dance in the view.
They wave their flippers, a silly salute,
To the setting sun, ah what a hoot!

So if you're lost at dusk's embrace,
Join the creatures in this happy space.
The ocean calls with a laugh and sigh,
As the sun waves on, bidding goodbye.

The Pulse of the Shore

The crabs dance to the beat,
Shells clatter in the heat.
Seagulls dive with great flair,
Snatching snacks from the air.

The waves hum a silly tune,
While starfish sing at noon.
Jellyfish float and sway,
In their own wobbly way.

Children giggle with glee,
Chasing surf like a flea.
Sandcastles rise up tall,
Then tumble with a call.

A beach ball rolls away,
Chased by a dog at play.
Laughter echoes and roars,
As joy spills on the shores.

Memories in the Mist

Seashells whisper secrets near,
Caught in laughter, full of cheer.
A pirate's hat flops askew,
Worn by one who's lost, it's true!

Fog rolls in with a silly grin,
A seahorse tries to swim in.
Mermaids giggle, tails on view,
Tail swaps lead to quite the brew.

The sandman's jokes, oh what fun,
Under the sweltering sun.
With each wave, a story shared,
Of silly fish who've always dared.

As twilight drapes its veil of dreams,
The ocean fancies glimmering beams.
All is merry, silly, bright,
In the mist where laughs take flight.

Fishermen's Fantasies

Bobbers float like silly hats,
Fishermen argue with their cats.
Baited hooks, but what a sight,
Fish swim off in pure delight!

One old man claims to boast,
Caught a shark, not just a ghost.
His pals chuckle, take their bets,
The fish with tales, no regrets.

Lines tangled in the breeze,
Catch of the day turns to tease.
A minnow rides a dolphin's back,
Making fishers' hopes turn black.

The net's a web of wild flair,
As fish giggle without a care.
They swim away, with cheeky laughs,
Leaving behind the fishermen's gaffs.

Reflecting the Dusk

The sun dips low, a clownish face,
Colors dance in a fiery embrace.
Seagulls gather in a fuss,
Who gets the last crumb? Oh, what a plus!

The ocean mimics the sky's show,
Reflecting giggles where sea breezes blow.
Crabs settle down, tired from the jest,
While fish flip and twirl, not a moment to rest.

All the sunbathers wave goodbye,
To hues of peach, to cotton candy sky.
The wind whispers secrets of the tide,
Of the giggly adventures, side by side.

As night hugs the land with a tickle,
Stars twinkle like fireflies in a sickle.
The humor of dusk, a playful tease,
Bringing dreams and laughter with the breeze.

Shadows on the Shimmering Sand

Twirling in the sun, my hat flew away,
A crab took it home, what a fine cabaret!
Seagulls laughed loudly, played tricks with the tide,
While I chased my headwear with my lost sense of pride.

A beach ball bounced high, then popped in a flash,
The kids all cheered loudly, then started to splash.
I slipped on that water, took quite the dive,
The ocean just chuckled, said, "Aren't you alive?"

A sunburned dog danced, chasing his tail,
His owner just sighed, "He has a grand sail!"
With cooler in tow, they strolled by so bold,
I offered my sunscreen, but he took my gold.

The ice cream truck rolled, a jingle so sweet,
I rushed to the line, fell flat on my feet.
The flavor I got was a flop and a mess,
But I wore it with pride — ain't life such a jest?

Love Among the Gulls

A couple got cozy while snacking on fries,
But gulls swooped down, oh, what a surprise!
They stole all the goodies, a feathered buffet,
The lovers just blushed, said, "Well, that's our day!"

She tossed them a morsel, he aimed for her heart,
But the birds squawked loudly, played their own part.
With laughter and crumbs, they flailed to take wing,
While love soared above — well, sort of a fling.

Then came a wise pelican, wise in disguise,
He winked at the couple, said, "Listen to cries!"
"For every lost fry, there's a seagull in sight,
Just love through the chaos, you'll be alright!"

They chuckled and shared, as the gulls dined with glee,
The joy of companionship, a sight to see.
Sandcastles crumbled, yet nothing was wrong,
For love at the beach is where hearts belong.

Voyage of the Forgotten Seas

Set sail on a rubber duck, plump and bright,
We paddled through waves, giggling with delight.
The compass confused, pointed straight to the shore,
But anchors don't do much when you're wanting to explore.

We found treasure chests filled with old sunscreen,
And bottles of rumors from a time far unseen.
A map drawn in ketchup with fries as the key,
We'll stake our claim here, in this kiddie spree!

Fish wore sunglasses, took sunbaths in glee,
While mermaids debated who's bounciest free.
We waved to the dolphins, who seemed in a cheer,
Said, "Don't forget your floaties, adventurers dear!"

As the skies began darkening, we laughed through the night,
Imagining sea monsters — all scared of our might.
But at the dock, we stumbled, with giggles in tow,
The voyage was wild; let's never say no!

Serendipity of the Coast

A clam in the sand wore a sassy little grin,
He challenged my sandals — said, "How do you swim?"
With waves rolling gently, they both found their beat,
As I laughed at their banter, life felt so sweet.

A surfboard was hidden below a bright towel,
And I tripped over it — made a face like an owl!
The ocean just giggled, with joy in its foam,
And I rolled in the surf, made the sea feel like home.

Fish tried to jump ropes, some tangled in tears,
While crabs played the drums, full of musical cheers.
A picnic unfolded with snacks flying high,
Only to land softly on a sun-baked pie.

Seagulls not shy, took the crust way too quick,
Then I chased after them, armed with my stick.
And as the sun set, with a wink and a dance,
We laughed at the memories, lost in our chance.

The Harmony of Saltwater and Sky

The seagulls dance and squawk a tune,
While crabs in shells play hide and seek!
A jellyfish floats, thinking it's a balloon,
As waves tickle toes every week.

Sandcastles rise, then tumble down,
With moats filled with giggles, not fear!
The tide pulls in, turns frowns to a crown,
And laughter blends with the salty cheer.

Fishes wear sunglasses, oh what a sight,
While seaweed sways like it's at a ball!
The beach umbrella flaps, giving a fright,
As it runs away—do we chase or just call?

Shells whisper secrets that make us grin,
Of mermaids and pirates with hats far too big.
We build our dreams, let the joy sink in,
As crabs do the conga, each one dressed in swig.

Lullabies of the Rolling Surf

The waves begin their nightly hum,
While surfers snooze on their boards—oh dear!
Two dolphins giggle, a mischief some,
As they sneak past snoring with great cheer.

Stars twinkle softly above the bay,
While a clam sings off-key, quite the show!
Sea turtles yawn and swim away,
Leaving jellyfish to steal the glow.

Seashells collect laughs from all around,
As crabs try to dance but just trip on air!
Sandcastles giggle with every sound,
As they crumble beneath the moon's soft stare.

The tide pulls back, but don't you fret,
Fish wear pajamas—it's quite a sight!
With sleepy waves and joy to be met,
We'll dream of the sea until morning light.

Mystic Currents of the Blue Abyss

Deep in the water, a whale may sing,
Not tunes of love, but a jolly jig!
A crab plays a sax, such a funny thing,
While turtles spin tales—oh what a gig!

Schools of fish wear party hats, it's true,
They swirl in a frenzy, not caring who sees!
A shark does the cha-cha, a marvelous view,
While octopuses giggle and tickle the breeze.

Pirate ships sail with sails made of cheese,
The waves can't stop rolling on with such grace!
Giant seaweed dances in a light tease,
As treasure chests open, all smiles on each face.

The ocean's a stage under starlit skies,
Where turtles and fishes join in the fun!
With bright little bubbles that giggle and rise,
The depths are alive, what a night to run!

A Tapestry of Seashell Stories

Gather 'round shells with tales to impart,
Of pirate ghosts and mermaid affairs!
Each one a story, a funny twist starts,
The conch tells jokes, and the barnacle shares.

Sand dollars giggle, oh what a thrill,
They flip in the sun, playing tag with the breeze!
Starfish tell secrets, with a wink and a chill,
As sand crabs compete in a race—oh please!

A fish with a mustache recites poetry,
As clams clap their shells in rhythm divine!
The laughter resounds like a grand jubilee,
While whales cheer on, with a deep, booming line.

Every splash tells a joke, every wave is a smile,
Bubbles escape, and we're all in a fit!
Together we cherish this wild, wavy style,
As the sea spins its yarns, and we can't help but admit!

Tales from the Shells

Upon the sands, a crab wore pants,
He danced around, gave folks a chance.
A starfish waved, all five of its hands,
Said, "Join my party, forget your plans!"

A clam exclaimed, "I'm a musical pro!"
With pearls as drums, they stole the show.
Seagulls laughed, fluttered to and fro,
While fish below went with the flow.

An octopus slipped, oh what a sight,
He tried to juggle, but lost his might.
"Next time," he grinned, "I'll get it right!"
And all joined in, beneath the daylight.

From shells they tell, these tales of fun,
In a world where laughter's never done.
So if you stroll, and hear a pun,
Know nature's humor has just begun.

Echoes of Ocean Dreams

A dolphin danced with a beach ball wide,
While seaweed swayed, like it was a ride.
A fish in a bow tie, oh what a pride,
Shimmied with flair, how the others cried!

The waves whispered jokes with a foamy laugh,
As two crabs argued over a seashell staff.
"I found it first!" went the little half,
But soon they both took a picture for the graph.

A whale told tales of a ship's cheeky cat,
Who swam with a seal, wearing a hat.
They splashed in a circle, what a silly spat,
As gulls sang tunes, full of chit and chitchat.

In this watery world, bright bubbles gleam,
Where laughter floats just like a dream.
Remember to smile, join the stream,
And share in the joy, it's a funny theme.

Beneath the Sunlit Surface

Beneath the waves, in a colorful groove,
A snail on a surfboard began to move.
"Hang ten!" he called, with style to prove,
While jellyfish glowed, eager to improve.

A sea cucumber, with dreams of the stage,
Said, "Watch me dance, turn the ocean page!"
But tripped on a rock, poor thing was in rage,
As fish laughed aloud, nothing to gauge.

A grouper in glasses read lines from a book,
While plankton cheered from every nook.
"What's the punchline?" asked one little cook,
And all fell over—what a silly look!

In the shimmering depths, where bubble paths twine,
Every creature's a star, waiting to shine.
With quirks and giggles, they all intertwine,
Creating a scene that's simply divine.

Dancers in the Sand

Under the sun, on a beach so grand,
A hermit crab wore a shiny band.
"Let's start a conga!" He waved his hand,
And soon all the creatures began to stand.

A seagull swooped in, with a flair so bright,
"Watch my moves!" as it took to flight.
A clam joined in, without any fright,
And the show went on, pure delight!

The tide pulled back, but they didn't care,
With flip-flopped turtles having a pair.
A sand dollar rolled—oh what a fair,
As laughter rubbed off, light as the air.

Down by the shore, bygone not a chance,
For all creatures, big and small, join the dance.
With a wave and a smile, they take their stance,
In a world where joy is the perfect romance.

Luminous Paths in the Ocean's Heart

I danced with a crab, he wore a hat,
He claimed he was the coolest of all chat!
A dolphin laughed, flipping with glee,
Said, 'Join my party, it's under the sea!'

A starfish told tales, all sticky and bright,
Of treasure maps hidden, oh what a sight!
The octopus winked, ink spilling like dreams,
"I'm just here for fun, or so it seems!"

Fish in tuxedos swam past with a glide,
They threw a great ball, oh what a ride!
With seaweed confetti and shells on the floor,
Who knew the ocean had plenty in store?

So let's raise a fin for the silliness here,
With laughter and bubbles, we have nothing to fear!
For beneath the waves where merriment flows,
Life's a grand party, as everyone knows!

Whispers of the Gentle Shoreline

Seagulls debated over crumbs and fries,
A clam claimed they tasted like real prize!
Shells held a meeting to plan a parade,
Coconut floats were the grand upgrade!

Sandcastles strutted, each sharper than the next,
With flags that declared, 'We're hardly vexed!'
A rogue crab danced, two steps to the left,
While sunbathers giggled at his little theft!

The tide rolled in wearing its big blue pants,
It said, 'Excuse me, do you want to dance?'
Frantic umbrellas caught wind like a kite,
Twisting and turning, what a silly sight!

As twilight descended and stars began to peek,
The moon cracked a joke, though the waves did speak!
So come join the fun, let's laugh and explore,
For mischief awaits on this gentle shore!

Whispers of the Tides

The waves had a secret behind their white foam,
They giggled and whispered, 'Come join our home!'
A fish in a bowtie recited great rhymes,
While crabs played charades, oh the funniest crimes!

They splashed with a wink, making bubbles so round,
Shiny and giggly, they danced without sound!
Anemones giggled in spite of their roots,
'We're the best dancers in colorful suits!'

A jellyfish twirled with umbrellas galore,
It said, 'I'm not stinging, just here for the score!'
The seaweed all cheered, their voices a blend,
With laughter so bright, it would never end!

When the tides pulled back, carrying delight,
The echo of laughter filled up the night.
So listen for whispers when the ocean sighs,
For humor is hiding beneath the blue skies!

Secrets Beneath the Waves

Beneath the bright surface, the fish sang a tune,
While turtles chilled out with their hats made of moon.
A mermaid complained, 'Stars won't align!'
But sea urchins nudged her, 'We're feeling just fine!'

An octopus juggled shells, quite the display!
'Can you top this?' asked the clam with a sway.
Everyone giggled, scales shimmering bright,
With bubbles that echoed, full of delight!

The sand made a joke, as it tickled a toe,
'Time to relax, let the good times flow!'
Whales chimed in, with a deep, booming cheer,
'We're the life of this party, so come persevere!'

When currents did swirl and the laughter grew loud,
The ocean's true joy felt both gentle and proud.
Dive in, take a swim in this wacky applause,
For secrets are waiting, just pause and because!

Mirage of the Horizon

A seagull stole my sandwich, oh dear,
It flew like it was hatching a plan,
I chased it down the beach in wild cheer,
But laughed at the sight of a clam's tan.

Waves crashed with giggles, splashing my feet,
As crabs did the moonwalk; quite absurd!
They danced in the sand, not missing a beat,
While I just sat back, utterly stirred.

A flip-flop sailed past in the salty breeze,
I wondered who lost their stylish grip.
My hat took flight, oh what a tease,
Maybe it joined in on the crabs' hip trip.

Sunset painted skies in shades of fun,
The horizon blinks—did it just wink?
The day may end, but the laughs weigh a ton,
And tomorrow holds more chaos, I think.

Footprints Under the Moonlight

In the silver glow where shadows play,
Footprints crisscross like lines on a map,
I wondered aloud, did I walk this way?
Or was it the dog? Oh, what a trap!

A crab waved a claw; it looked quite dapper,
And made a fine jest of my lost-shoe chase.
The stars overhead began to stammer,
As I tripped on sand with all my grace.

Nearby, a couple fought over a snack,
Popcorn flung 'round like confetti at night.
I snagged a piece, planning a sneak attack,
But their laughter turned my heist into fright.

Waves giggled softly, tickling my toes,
As I danced like a fool on that moonlit stage.
Who cares about fame or a grandiose prose?
I'm here for the fun, not for a wage!

Crystals of the Sea

On the beach, I stumbled on treasures galore,
Shells sparkling like jewels beneath my feet.
I pocketed a rock and two shells for sure,
But stopped for a moment, my thoughts in retreat.

A jellyfish waved—was it saying hello?
Or urging me to join its fancy ball?
I grinned and spun, but I tripped on a row,
Of sandcastles crumbling, they surely took a fall.

The tide tickled my toes, made them all tingle,
As I searched for pearls—but only found tacos.
With each goofy step, my laughter would jingle,
Even sea stars seemed to share in my woes.

The sunset dazzled like crystal confetti,
And dolphins joined in, leaping with glee.
With laughter still echoing, spirits were ready,
Tomorrow I'll search for more gems by the sea.

Sirens' Songs at Twilight

As daylight faded, the mermaids appeared,
Their songs sounded like tunes from a used jukebox.
But they sang of tacos, and I bit back a sneer,
Picturing them on seaside lunch with a fox.

They swirled through the foam, with hair in a whirl,
Offering laughs, yet I stayed on the shore.
One winked at me—oh, what a surreal girl!
I had to admit; I was wanting some more.

Their glittery tails flashed under soft light,
As they teased and played like it was a game.
Not sure if I'd join them in the cool night,
But I waved back and shouted: "Let's make it a flame!"

Their giggles rang out, a whimsical tune,
While I twirled in sand, sandwiched between jests.
The song of the sea on a crescent moon,
Laughter and magic; oh, how it begets!

Portraits of Horizon

A crab in a hat, quite absurd,
Struts on the sand, quite undeterred.
He claims he's the king, but we all know,
He's just after fries from the picnic show.

Seagulls gather, plotting a heist,
Stealing our snacks, oh what a sight!
They squawk and they dive, with mischief galore,
While beachgoers gasp, then laugh on the shore.

A dog in shades, lounging with flair,
Turns heads as he barks, for all to beware.
He's the lifeguard, or so he insists,
As he chases a wave, but it's a miss!

With sandcastles toppled by nimble tides,
The royal palace of dreams quickly slides.
Yet laughter persists amidst all the mess,
In a kingdom of folly, who could care less?

Breath of the Sea

Waves bubble like soda, a fizzy delight,
Where fish wear bow ties, quite the weird sight.
A dolphin with shades makes a splashy debut,
As beachgoers cheer for the oceanic view.

Seashells are treasures, or so they proclaim,
But most are just junk—what a funny game!
A conch shell lies, claiming to speak,
But only echoes of laughter, so unique.

The tide rolls in, with glitter and foam,
While crabs do the cha-cha, feeling at home.
They dance with the waves in a hilarious spree,
Oh, the humor that lurks beneath the sea!

With sunglasses on, a beach ball they chase,
Who knew crustaceans could keep such a pace?
As the sun dips low, they bow in style,
For in their silly antics, we all find a smile!

The Dance of Moonlit Waters

Under twilight's gaze, the waves pull a prank,
Turtles in tuxedos parade the plank.
A starfish in slippers attempts a waltz,
While dancers from shells spin, oh what a pulse!

Moonbeams flicker, casting shadows about,
A fish doing flips, while the crab shouts out.
"Join us!" he calls, with a snap and a snap,
And we all giggle at the nighttime flap.

The seaweed sways, like a hair gone wild,
As it tickles the toes of the beach baby child.
Under the stars, every creature ignites,
In rhythm and laughter, all hearts feel light.

A glow from the waters, the laughter won't cease,
As jellyfish jiggle like bouncing caprice.
In this oceanic ballroom, we find our own tune,
Forget all the worries, just dance by the moon!

Diary of the Shorelines

In the diary of sand, stories are scribed,
Of seagulls who argue, competing for jibes.
Crabs take notes while dodging the flares,
Of sunscreen mishaps and epic beach chairs.

With each passing wave, new secrets unfold,
Of mermaids who bubble with treasures untold.
Each fish has a tale, a yarn or a joke,
Making giggles arise from the driest of folk.

Footprints in sand, a map of the fun,
Leading to laughter, where everyone runs.
A parrot squawks news, a comedian star,
"Guess who's coming to dinner? It's a jellyfish bazaar!"

In this sandy journal, the entries grow wide,
With tales of the tide, and the joy we can't hide.
From laughter to mischief, the shoreline agrees,
Adventure awaits where the land meets the seas!

www.ingramcontent.com/pod-product-compliance
Lightning Source LLC
Chambersburg PA
CBHW072128070526
44585CB00016B/1581